FUNDAMENTAL PHONICS

by
Kathryn Wheeler
and
Meish Goldish

Cover Illustration
by
Mia Tavonatti

Inside Illustrations
by
Ann Lutnicki

Publishers
Instructional Fair • TS Denison
Grand Rapids, Michigan 49544

About the Authors

Kathryn Wheeler is an editor at
Instructional Fair and has written
stories and poems for children.
Meish Goldish has published over
30 books for children, in a range
that includes fiction, nonfiction,
and poetry.

Credits

Authors: Kathryn Wheeler and Meish Goldish
Cover Illustration: Mia Tavonatti
Inside Illustration: Ann Lutnicki
Project Director: Kathryn Wheeler
Editors: Wendy Roh Jenks and Linda Triemstra
Page Design: Pat Geasler

Standard Book Number: 1-56822-837-6
"Fun"damental Phonics—Grade K
Copyright © 1999 by Ideal•Instructional Fair Publishing Group
a division of Tribune Education
Grand Rapids, Michigan 49544

Table of Contents

Answer Key In Middle of Book

Circle the words that start with *B b*. Say the sound.

Bob's Bike

Bob bought a bike,
A beautiful bike,
With big baskets on both sides
They hold baseballs and bats,
Books, boxes, and bags,
Now Bob has no room for rides!

4

Color the pictures that start with the sound you hear at the beginning of .

IF0360 *"Fun"damental Phonics*

Circle the words that start with C c. Say the sound.

Come, Cozy Cat

Cute, cozy cat,

Curled up in a corner

Care to come out for a break?

Cute, cozy cat,

I'm calling! Come!

In your cup is a cool carrot cake.

IF0360 *"Fun"damental Phonics*

Draw a line from Cozy Cat to each picture that starts with the sound you hear at the beginning of .

7

Circle the words that start with *D d.* Say the sound.

Dinner Dishes

Dinner is done,
The dishes are dirty,
Doing each dish is a chore!
Do be a dear
And help do the dishes—
Don't dare to dash out the door!

© Instructional Fair • TS Denison   IF0360 *"Fun"damental Phonics*

Circle the pictures that start with the sound you hear at the beginning of  .

Circle the words that start with *F f.* Say the sound.

Foxy Fox

Foxy Fox found fifty figs

In a forest far away.

The figs were full,

The figs were fat,

The figs were falling,

Fancy that!

Circle the picture on each line that starts with the sound you hear at the beginning of 🐸 .

1.

2.

3.

IF0360 *"Fun"damental Phonics*

Circle the words that start with *G g*. Say the sound.

Goat and Goose
A-Gobbling

Goat got the garbage

By the garage.

Goose got the goodies

By the garden gate.

Goat and Goose

Gobbled their goods

Before it was too late!

IF0360 *"Fun"damental Phonics*

On each line, circle the picture that starts with the sound you hear at the beginning of .

1. goes through the   .

2.  has a friend,   .

3.  and  found food in the

 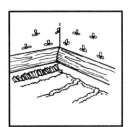 .

© Instructional Fair • TS Denison   IF0360 *"Fun"damental Phonics*

Circle the words that start with *H h*. Say the sound.

Helping Hands

Helping hands!

Hey! Hey, help!

Hurry to this hill!

I'm hanging here

Please come near.

Grab my hand

And help me stand.

IF0360 *"Fun"damental Phonics*

Cut out *H h* letters from magazines or newspapers. Glue them inside the heart.

Circle the words that start with *J j*. Say the sound.

Jeep Ride

Jungle-bumble jeep ride,

Jelly and jam,

Bounce with a jolt and a jeer.

Jam on my jacket!

Jelly on my jeans!

It's sticky and I can't steer!

IF0360 *"Fun"damental Phonics*

Circle the picture on each line that starts with the sound you hear at the beginning of .

1. I ride in a

2. I wear a

3. I eat

IF0360 *"Fun"damental Phonics*

Circle the words that start with *K k*. Say the sound.

Kangaroo Kick

Kangaroo, kick a kitchen sink,

Kick a kettle, a kite,

Or a key.

Kick a kerchief or a king,

Kick any kind of thing,

Kangaroo.

Just don't kick me!

© Instructional Fair • TS Denison IF0360 *"Fun"damental Phonics*

Draw a line from Kangaroo to each picture that starts with the sound you hear at the beginning of  .

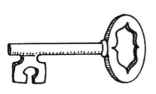

IF0360 *"Fun"damental Phonics*

Circle the words that start with *L l*. Say the sound.

Lip-Smacking Treats

Licorice whips and large lollipops,

Here are some yellow lemon drops

Hurry now—

Better be quick!

Which lip-smacking treat

Will you pick?

IF0360 *"Fun"damental Phonics*

Pick your *L* treats! Circle the pictures that start with the sound you hear at the beginning of .

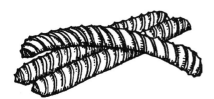

IF0360 *"Fun"damental Phonics*

Circle the words that start with *M m*. Say the sound.

Monday Morning March-Along

Monday morning,

Month of May,

Many mice march on their way

As Mister Mike milks the cow,

And Mister Cat moans, "Meow!"

22

Color the pictures that start with the sound you hear at the beginning of  .

Circle the words that start with *N n*. Say the sound.

Never a Noise

No one is here,
Nobody's near,
No nice neighbor next door.
Never a noise,
Nothing to notice,
Noon to night,
What a bore!

© Instructional Fair • TS Denison   IF0360 *"Fun"damental Phonics*

Color the pictures that start with the sound you hear at the beginning of .

Write your name:

IF0360 *"Fun"damental Phonics*

Circle the words that start with *P p*. Say the sound.

Picnic in the Park

Picnic in the park,

Perfect sky,

Peanuts, popcorn,

Piece of pie!

Picnic in the park,

Pass the day,

Parties, a parade,

And pool play!

IF0360 *"Fun"damental Phonics*

Time for a ! Circle the pictures that start with the sound you hear at the beginning of .

IF0360 *"Fun"damental Phonics*

Circle the words that start with Q q. Say the sound.

Quacking Queen Duck

Queen Duck quacks at quiet quail,

Some quarters and a quilt.

Queen Duck's quack is really quite loud.

She can be heard above the crowd!

Color each picture on a that starts with the Q sound.

IF0360 *"Fun"damental Phonics*

Circle the words that start with *R r.* Say the sound.

The Race

Rooster and Rabbit raced in the rain,

Round the Red Road bend.

Running! Running!

From river to ranch,

To reach Raccoon at the end!

IF0360 *"Fun"damental Phonics*

Circle the words that start with the sound you hear at the beginning of .

1.  ran in the

 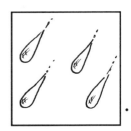 .

2. ran with

  .

3.  went to meet

  .

IF0360 *"Fun"damental Phonics*

Circle the words that start with *S s*. Say the sound.

Sipping Soup

Super Sarah sips her soup

With a super sort of spoon.

Its super size is so big,

Super Sarah's done too soon!

IF0360 *"Fun"damental Phonics*

Make lunch! Draw a line from Super Sarah to each word that starts with the sound you hear at the beginning of ⬚ .

IF0360 "Fun"damental Phonics

Circle the words that start with *T t*. Say the sound.

Tiptoe Turtle

Tiny turtle,
Tiptoe to town,
Tiptoe up,
Tiptoe down.
Tiny turtle,
Tiptoe away,
Tiptoe tomorrow,
Tiptoe today.

IF0360 *"Fun"damental Phonics*

Where did Tiny Turtle go? Circle the words that start with the sound you hear at the beginning of .

1.  went past a   .

2. saw a   .

3. went to   .

IF0360 *"Fun"damental Phonics*

Circle the words that start with *V v*. Say the sound.

Visiting

In the valley,
On the vine,
Vegetables are very fine!
Visit the valley,
Visit the vine,
Visit the vegetables very fine!

IF0360 *"Fun"damental Phonics*

Answer Key

"Fun"damental Phonics

Grade K

Circle the words that start with B b. Say the sound.

Bob's Bike

Bob bought a bike,
A beautiful bike,
With big baskets on both sides
They hold baseballs and bats,
Books, boxes, and bags,
Now Bob has no room for rides!

© Instructional Fair • TS Denison   4   IF0360 "Fun"damental Phonics

---

Recognizing /b/   ABC

Color the pictures that starts with the sound you hear at the beginning of

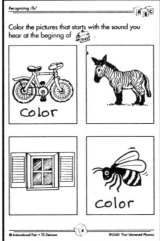

Color

Color

© Instructional Fair • TS Denison   5   IF0360 "Fun"damental Phonics

---

ABC

Circle the words that start with C c. Say the sound.

Come, Cozy Cat

Cute, Cozy Cat,
Curled up in a corner
Care to come out for a break?
Cute, Cozy Cat,
I'm calling! Come!
In your cup is a cool carrot cake.

© Instructional Fair • TS Denison   6   IF0360 "Fun"damental Phonics

---

Recognizing /c/   ABC

Draw a line from Cozy Cat to each picture that starts with the sound you hear at the beginning of

© Instructional Fair • TS Denison   7   IF0360 "Fun"damental Phonics

---

ABC

Circle the words that start with D d. Say the sound.

Dinner Dishes

Dinner is done,
The dishes are dirty,
Doing each dish is a chore!
Do be a dear
And help do the dishes—
Don't dare to dash out the door!

© Instructional Fair • TS Denison   8   IF0360 "Fun"damental Phonics

---

Recognizing /d/   ABC

Circle the pictures that start with the sound you hear at the beginning of

© Instructional Fair • TS Denison   9   IF0360 "Fun"damental Phonics

---

Circle the words that start with *F f*. Say the sound.

Foxy Fox

Foxy Fox found fifty figs
In a forest far away.
The figs were full,
The figs were fat,
The figs were falling,
Fancy that!

Circle the picture on each line that starts with the sound you hear at the beginning of ___ .

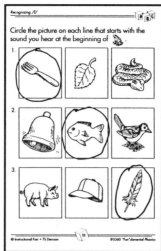

1.
2.
3.

Circle the words that start with *G g*. Say the sound.

**Goat and Goose
A-Gobbling**

Goat got the garbage
By the garage.
Goose got the goodies
By the garden gate.
Goat and Goose
Gobbled their goods
Before it was too late!

On each line, circle the picture that starts with the sound you hear at the beginning of ___ .

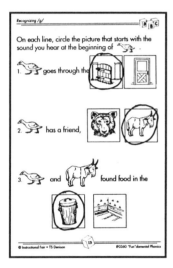

1. ___ goes through the ___

2. ___ has a friend,

3. ___ and ___ found food in the

Circle the words that start with *H h*. Say the sound.

**Helping
Hands**

Helping hands!
Hey! Hey help!
Hurry to this hill!
I'm hanging here
Please come near.
Grab my hand
And help me stand.

Cut out *H h* letters from magazines or newspapers. Glue them inside the heart.

Letters
pasted
here.

Circle the words that start with *J j*. Say the sound.

Jeep Ride

Jingle-bumble jeep ride,
Jelly and jam,
Bounce with a jolt and a jar.
Jam on my jacket!
Jelly on my jeans!
It's sticky and I can't steer!

Circle the picture on each line that starts with the sound you hear at the beginning of ___

1. I ride in a

2. I wear a

3. I eat

Circle the words that start with *K k*. Say the sound.

Kangaroo Kick

Kangaroo, kick a kitchen sink,
Kick a kettle, a kite,
Or a key.
Kick a kerchief or a king,
Kick any kind of thing,
Kangaroo.
Just don't kick me!

Draw a line from Kangaroo to each picture that starts with the sound you hear at the beginning of 🦘.

Circle the words that start with L l. Say the sound.

Lip-Smacking Treats

Licorice whips and large lollipops,
Here are some yellow lemon drops
Hurry now—
Better be quick!
Which lip-smacking treat
Will you pick?

Pick your L treats! Circle the pictures that start with the sound you hear at the beginning of 🦁.

Circle the words that start with M m. Say the sound.

Monday Morning March-Along

Monday morning,
Month of May,
Many mice march on their way
As Mister Mike milks the cow,
And Mister Cat moans, "Meow!"

Color the pictures that start with the sound you hear at the beginning of 🎈.

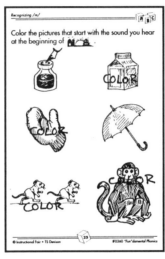

Circle the words that start with N n. Say the sound.

Never a Noise

No one is here,
Nobody's near,
No nice neighbor next door.
Never a noise,
Nothing to notice,
Noon tonight,
What a bore!

Color the pictures that start with the sound you hear at the beginning of 🪺.

Write your name:

Circle the words that start with P p. Say the sound.

Picnic in the Park

Picnic in the park,
Perfect sky,
Peanuts, popcorn,
Piece of pie!
Picnic in the park,
Pass the day,
Parties, a parade,
And pool play!

Time for a 🥧! Circle the pictures that start with the sound you hear at the beginning of 🥧.

Quacking Queen Duck

Queen Duck quacks at quiet quail,
Some quarters and a quilt.
Queen Duck's quack is really quite loud.
She can be heard above the crowd!

Color each picture on a [quilt] that starts with the Q sound.

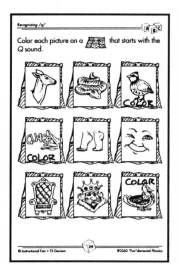

The Race

Rooster and Rabbit raced in the rain,
Round the Red Road bend.
Running! Running!
From river to ranch,
To reach Raccoon at the end!

Circle the words that start with the sound you hear at the beginning of [rooster].

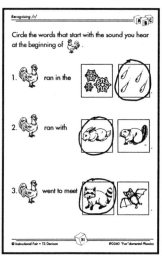

1. [rooster] ran in the
2. [rooster] ran with
3. [rooster] went to meet

Circle the words that start with S s. Say the sound.

Sipping Soup

Super Sarah sips her soup
With a super sort of spoon.
Its super size is so big,
Super Sarah's done too soon!

Make lunch! Draw a line from Super Sarah to each word that starts with the sound you hear at the beginning of [sandwich].

Circle the words that start with T t. Say the sound.

Tiptoe Turtle

Tiny Turtle,
Tiptoe to town,
Tiptoe up,
Tiptoe down.
Tiny Turtle,
Tiptoe away,
Tiptoe tomorrow,
Tiptoe today.

Where did Tiny Turtle go? Circle the words that start with the sound you hear at the beginning of [turtle].

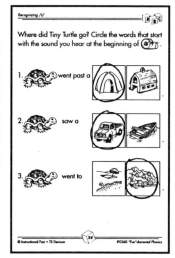

1. [turtle] went past a
2. [turtle] saw a
3. [turtle] went to

Circle the words that start with V v. Say the sound.

Visiting

In the valley,
On the vine,
Vegetables are very fine!
Visit the valley,
Visit the vine,
Visit the vegetables very fine!

Make a garden! Color the words that start with the sound you hear at the beginning of 🍶.

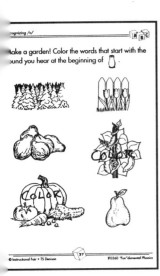

Circle the words that start with W w. Say the sound.

Watching Out My Window

Watching out my window
On a wonderful day
I can see
A woman
With a wagon
Walking my way.

Circle each [window] that has pictures starting with the sound you hear at the beginning of 🪱.

Circle the words that start or end with X x. Say the sound.

Xavier the Fox

Xavier the fox
Sat on a large box
Which broke as he tried to relax
Xavier got OK
To help fix the box
And that was the end of that!

Note: Because there are so few words that begin with the x sound, this poem involves ending sounds. Your child may need additional help with this page.

Cut out X x letters from magazines or newspapers. Glue them on the boxes.

Circle the words that start with Y y. Say the sound.

Yak in the Yard

Look! Look!
Over yonder in the yard.
Yes! Yes!
There's a yak
standing guard,
Yawning a great
big yawn.
Think he'll nap here
on our lawn?

Circle the picture on each line that starts with the sound you hear at the beginning of 🐑.

1. Where is 🦬 ?

2. What is 🦬 doing?

3. Which toy does 🦬 like?

Circle the words that start with Z z. Say the sound.

Zooming Zebra

Zoom off to the zoo
To see a zebra with stripes
And other animals of all types.
Zoom off to the zoo
To see an ostrich's plume.
Zoom off to the zoo.
Zoom, zoom, zoom!

Draw a line from the 🦓 to the words that start with the sound you hear at the beginning of 🦓.

Circle the words that start with A a. Say the short a sound.

Family Album

Annie! Come here!
Come! Come!
Look at this picture
In the family album.
Look, it's Annie
Eating apple pie.
Wish we had some!
Oh, my!

Recognizing short / a /

Circle the pictures which start with the sound that you hear at the beginning of

Circle the words that start with E e. Say the short e sound.

Exercise

The elves liked to do
Each exercise,
Much to the
Shoemaker's surprise!
So exhausted was
Elmer Elf
He couldn't even climb
Up to his shelf!

Recognizing short / e /

Color each picture which starts with the sound that you hear at the beginning of

Circle the words that start with I i. Say the short i sound.

In an Instant

In an instant
An inchworm inches near.
In an instant
I can disappear!
In an instant
An insect digs a ditch.
In an instant
You can scratch an itch!

Recognizing short / i /

Draw a line from each letter i to a picture that starts with the sound you hear at the beginning of

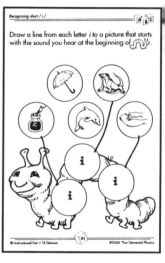

Circle the words that start with O o. Say the short o sound.

Otter

Otter likes to play
With many things
Like olives, octagons,
And big round rings.
Otter eats urchins,
Abalone, and fish.
You won't see an
Omelet on his dish!

Recognizing short / o /

Circle each picture that starts with the sound you hear at the beginning of

Circle the words that start with U u. Say the short u sound.

Umbrellas Up

An umbrella goes up.
An umbrella goes down.
People hide under umbrellas
All over town.
It's quite a funny sight
To watch people frown,
When gusts of strong wind
Turn umbrellas upside-down.

© Instructional Fair • TS Denison

IF0360 "Fun"damental Phonics

Cut out *U u* letters from magazines or newspapers.
Glue them on the umbrella.

Vowel Roundup

Draw a line from each vowel to the picture that starts with the short-vowel sound.

A a

E e

I i

O o

U u

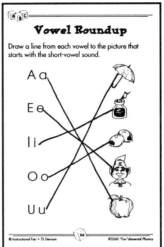

Draw a line from each picture to its 🏠 !
The letter for each sound is on the door.

What Doesn't Belong?

Put an **X** through the picture on each line that doesn't start with the same sound as the others.

1.

2.

3.

Put an **X** through the picture that doesn't start with the same sound.

4.

5.

6.

Lost and Found

Draw a line from each poem character to the picture that starts with the same sound.

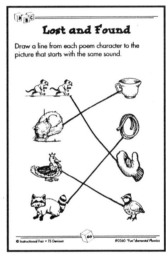

Match the beginning sounds.

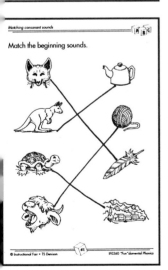

Fox's Fence

Draw a line to put every *F f* picture inside Fox's fence!

Now pack Bob's bike! Draw a line from the bike to each picture that starts with the *B b* sound.

Goose Gathers

Help Goose gather. Draw a line from Goose to the pictures that start with the *G g* sound.

Knowing /g/ from /k/ and /d/ from /t/

shops in town. Circle the pictures that start with the *T t* sound. See what he buys!

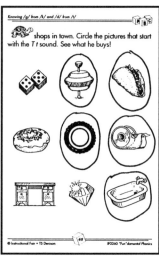

Rhyme Time

Circle the rhyming words in each line.

1.
2.
3.

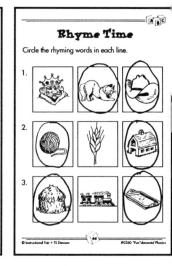

Matching rhyming words

Circle the rhyming words in each line.

4.
5.
6.

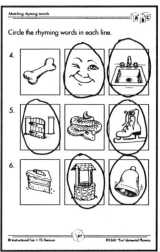

Finish the Poem

Circle the rhyming words that complete the poem. Ask an adult to help you read and choose the words.

There once was a ___ who brought

home a ___ .

She put it in a ___ with a whole

___ of ___

Her ___ would not eat it, but sat on

the ___ ,

So the ___ ate supper with her fat

___ ___ !

Finding rhyming words

Circle the rhyming words that finish the poem. Ask an adult to help you.

We know a ___

Who will never ___

He rides the circus ___

In the ___

And shares his ___

With a ___

When his ___ fell ___

He still did not ___ !

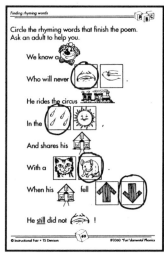

Find the "Un" Rhymes!

Find the word that does not rhyme in each line. Put an X on it.

1.
2.
3.

Recognizing rhyming words

Put an X on the word that does not rhyme in each line.

4.
5.
6.

Make a garden! Color the words that start with the sound you hear at the beginning of  .

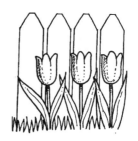

IF0360 *"Fun"damental Phonics*

Circle the words that start with *W w*. Say the sound

Watching Out
My Window

Watching out my window
On a wonderful day
I can see
A woman
With a wagon
Walking my way.

IF0360 *"Fun"damental Phonics*

Circle each  that has pictures starting with the sound you hear at the beginning of .

IF0360 "Fun"damental Phonics

Circle the words that start or end with *X x*. Say the sound.

Xavier the Fox

Xavier the fox

Sat on a large box

Which broke as he tried to relax.

Xavier got Ox

To help fix the box

And that was the end of that!

Note: Because there are so few words that begin with the **x** sound, this poem involves ending sounds. Your child may need additional help with this page.

IF0360 *"Fun"damental Phonics*

Cut out *X x* letters from magazines or newspapers.
Glue them on the boxes.

Circle the words that start with *Y y*. Say the sound.

Yak in the Yard

Look! Look!
Over yonder in the yard.
Yes! Yes!
There's a yak
standing guard,
Yawning a great
big yawn.
Think he'll nap here
on our lawn?

IF0360 *"Fun"damental Phonics*

Circle the picture on each line that starts with the sound you hear at the beginning of .

1. Where is ?

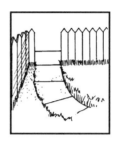 

2. What is  doing?

3. Which toy does like?

Circle the words that start with *Z z*. Say the sound.

Zooming Zebra

Zoom off to the zoo
To see a zebra with stripes
And other animals of all types.
Zoom off to the zoo
To see an ostrich's plume.
Zoom off to the zoo.
Zoom, zoom, zoom!

IF0360 *"Fun"damental Phonics*

Draw a line from the  to the words that start with the sound you hear at the beginning of  .

IF0360 *"Fun"damental Phonics*

Circle the words that start with *A a*. Say the short *a* sound.

Family Album

Annie! Come here!

Come! Come!

Look at this picture

In the family album.

Look, it's Annie

Eating apple pie.

Wish we had some!

Oh, my!

IF0360 *"Fun"damental Phonics*

Circle the pictures which start with the sound that you hear at the beginning of .

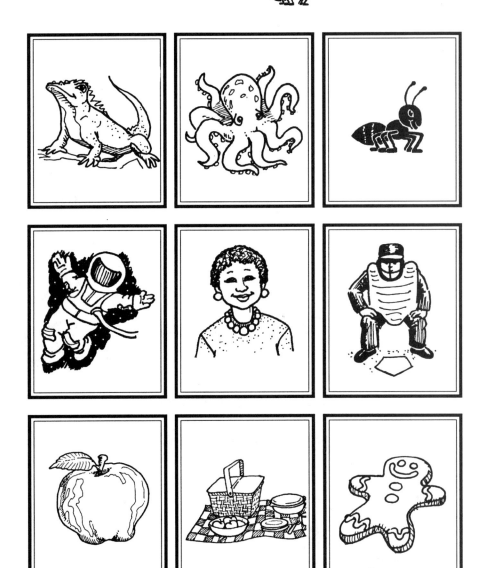

IF0360 *"Fun"damental Phonics*

Circle the words that start with *E e*. Say the short *e* sound.

Exercise

The elves liked to do
Each exercise,
Much to the
Shoemaker's surprise!
So exhausted was
Elmer Elf
He couldn't even climb
Up to his shelf!

© Instructional Fair • TS Denison   IF0360 *"Fun"damental Phonics*

Color each picture which starts with the sound that you hear at the beginning of .

49

Circle the words that start with *I i*. Say the short *i* sound.

In an Instant

In an instant

An inchworm inches near.

In an instant

It can disappear!

In an instant

An insect digs a ditch.

In an instant

You can scratch an itch!

© Instructional Fair • TS Denison   IF0360 *"Fun"damental Phonics*

Draw a line from each letter *i* to a picture that starts with the sound you hear at the beginning of

Circle the words that start with *O o*. Say the short *o* sound.

Otter

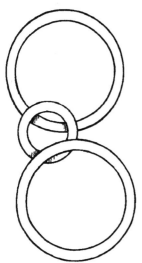

Otter likes to play
With many things
Like olives, octagons,
And big round rings.
Otter eats urchins,
Abalone, and fish.
You won't see an
Omelet on his dish!

 IF0360 *"Fun"damental Phonics*

Circle each picture that starts with the sound you hear at the beginning of  .

IF0360 "Fun"damental Phonics

Circle the words that start with *U u*. Say the short *u* sound.

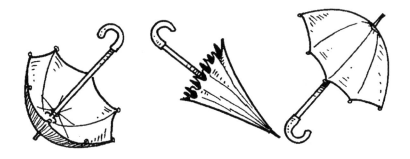

Umbrellas Up

An umbrella goes up.
An umbrella goes down.
People hide under umbrellas
All over town.
It's quite a funny sight
To watch people frown,
When gusts of strong wind
Turn umbrellas upside-down.

IF0360 *"Fun"damental Phonics*

Cut out *U u* letters from magazines or newspapers. Glue them on the umbrella.

© Instructional Fair • TS Denison

IF0360 *"Fun"damental Phonics*

Vowel Roundup

Draw a line from each vowel to the picture that starts with the short-vowel sound.

A a

E e

I i

O o

U u

IF0360 *"Fur."damental Phonics*

Draw a line from each picture to its !
The letter for each sound is on the door.

IF0360 *"Fun"damental Phonics*

What Doesn't Belong?

Put an **X** through the picture on each line that doesn't start with the same sound as the others.

1.

2.

3.
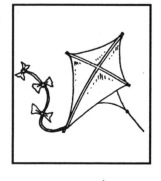 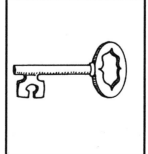 

IF0360 *"Fun"damental Phonics*

Put an **X** through the picture that doesn't start with the same sound.

4.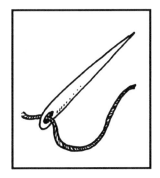

5.

6.

IF0360 *"Fun"damental Phonics*

Lost and Found

Draw a line from each poem character to the picture that starts with the same sound.

IF0360 *"Fun"damental Phonics*

Match the beginning sounds.

IF0360 *"Fun"damental Phonics*

Fox's Fence

Draw a line to put every *F f* picture inside Fox's fence!

IF0360 *"Fun"damental Phonics*

Now pack Bob's bike! Draw a line from the bike to each picture that starts with the *B b* sound.

IF0360 *"Fun"damental Phonics*

Goose Gathers

Help Goose gather. Draw a line from Goose to the pictures that start with the *G g* sound.

IF0360 *"Fun"damental Phonics*

 shops in town. Circle the pictures that start with the *T t* sound. See what he buys!

IF0360 *"Fun"damental Phonics*

Rhyme Time

Circle the rhyming words in each line.

1.

2.

3.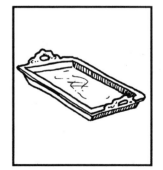

IF0360 *"Fun"damental Phonics*

Circle the rhyming words in each line.

4.
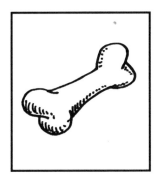  

5.
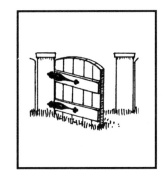  

6.

IF0360 *"Fun"damental Phonics*

Finish the Poem

Circle the rhyming words that complete the poem. Ask an adult to help you read and choose the words.

There once was a who brought

home a .

She put it in a with a whole

 of   !

Her would not eat it, but sat on

the  ,

So the ate supper with her fat

 !

Circle the rhyming words that finish the poem.
Ask an adult to help you.

We know a

Who will never   .

He rides the circus

In the   ,

And shares his

With a   .

When his fell

He <u>still</u> did not !

IF0360 *"Fun"damental Phonics*

Find the "Un" Rhymes!

Find the word that does <u>not</u>
rhyme in each line. Put an X on it.

1.

  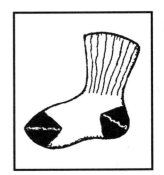

2.

 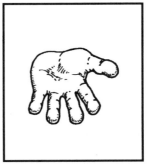 

3.

IF0360 "Fun'damental Phonics

Put an X on the word that does <u>not</u> rhyme in each line.

4.

5.
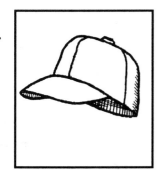
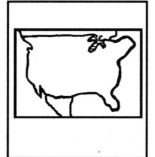

6.
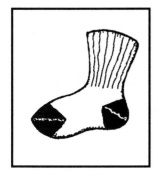

IF0360 *"Fun"damental Phonics*

Help-At-Home Activities

1. When playing with your child, hold up a toy and ask, "What sound does **ball** start with?" Be sure to pronounce the word clearly to help your child hear the sound.

2. In the supermarket check-out line, choose an object from your cart and ask, "What sound does **milk** start with?"

3. When reading a story, ask your child what sound begins the name of the main character. Find that same letter and sound in a word on each page.

4. At bedtime, ask your child to find one object in his/her room that begins with a sound you designate.

5. Make a set of picture cards from magazines or newspapers. Ask your child to identify the beginning sound of each word. Then have your child match two pictures that begin with the same sound.

6. Give your child a stack of old magazines. Select a word with a simple sound, such as "**ball**." Suggest that your child hunt for pictures that rhyme with the word you have chosen.

7. Have a scavenger hunt in your home. Ask your child to find one object that starts with a designated sound from each room.

8. Write down the names of your child's friends. Say each name and ask your child to identify the sound at the beginning of each name.

9. Go through the poems in this homework booklet and read each one out loud. Work with your child to find all the rhyming words in the poems.

© Instructional Fair • TS Denison

IF0360 *"Fun'damental Phonic*